Just the Facts
Cancer

Oliver Gillie

Heinemann Library
Chicago, Illinois

Customer Service 888-454-2279
Visit our website at www.heinemannlibrary.com

Produced by Monkey Puzzle Media
Designed by Jamie Asher
Originated by Ambassador Litho Ltd.
Printed and bound in China by South China Printing Company

08 07 06 05 04
10 9 8 7 6 5 4 3 2 1

Library of Congress Cataloging-in-Publication Data
A copy of the cataloging-in-publication data for this title is on file with the Library of Congress.
Cancer / Oliver Gillie
ISBN 1-4034-5144-3

Acknowledgments
The publishers would like to thank the following for permission to reproduce photographs:
Alamy pp. 1 (Mark Harmel), 11 (Popperfoto), 14 (Janine Weidel Photo library), 24 (Mark Harmel), 28 (ImageState), 41 (Stock Connections), 42 (Photofusion), 46 (ImageState); Corbis pp. 21 (Tom and Dee Ann McCarthy), 23 (David Butow/SABA); Mary Evans Picture Library p. 9; PA Photos p. 51 (Owen Humphreys); Science Photo Library pp. 4 (Geoff Tompkinson), 6–7 (Dr Gopal Murti), 8 (CC Studio), 12, 13 (Will and Deni McIntyre), 15 (Josh Sher), 16, 17 (Geoff Tompkinson), 18 (Mauro Fermariello), 19 (Mauro Fermariello), 25 (Mauro Fermariello), 26 (Simon Fraser/Royal Victoria Infirmary, Newcastle), 27, 29 (Dr P Marazzi), 30 (John Cole), 33 (Colin Cuthbert), 34 (Simon Fraser/Royal Victoria Infirmary, Newcastle), 35 (Colin Cuthbert), 37 (Simon Fraser), 38 (Philippe Plailly), 43 (Chris Priest), 49 (John Cole); Matthew Zachary p. 45.

Cover photograph: main image Corbis/ A. Kleschuck/Sygma; second image: Science Photo Library

The case studies in this book are based on factual information. In some case studies and elsewhere in this book, names or other personal information may have been changed or omitted in order to protect the privacy of the individuals concerned.

Contents

The Fight Against Cancer

Cancer is now the most common cause of death in developed countries. Cancer is feared because it seems to kill by stealth—appearing in otherwise healthy people and slowly reducing them to a pale shadow of their former selves. Progress in developing new treatments has been slow because there are so many different types of cancer, but thanks to medical progress, cancer can often be beaten.

"Harry Potter helped me get through some really hard and scary times. I sometimes think of Harry Potter and me as being kind of alike. He was forced into situations he could not control, and had to face an enemy he didn't know if he could beat. Harry Potter helped me to realize that with the love and support of the people around me, I could get better."

(Tyler Walton, Oaklyn, New Jersey)

Tyler's story

Cancer is rare in children, but Tyler Walton from Oaklyn, New Jersey, became ill with leukemia at the age of five. At first he seemed to be responding well to treatment. Most children are cured after two or three years, but in Tyler's case the disease returned worse than ever three and a half years later.

The cancer invaded Tyler's bones and his spinal cord. His whole body seemed to be under attack. For months he couldn't walk and his food was given to him through a tube. It seemed as bad as it could get. His parents asked themselves if they were doing the right thing by putting him through treatment that seemed worse than the disease.

Then doctors suggested a bone marrow transplant. Tyler's sister, Molly, was a perfect donor, because her bone marrow was a perfect match. So Tyler had a transfusion of Molly's bone marrow cells. After he had recovered, Tyler could once again do all the things other children could do, such as running, playing, and eating.

During his illness Tyler's parents read aloud to him from the book *Harry Potter and the Philosopher's Stone*. His mother Maureen got into bed with him and snuggled close while Tyler closed his eyes and listened. It was a special time for them when they escaped from drips and needles into a world of magic and adventure.

Left: A young cancer patient in a hospital.

What Is Cancer?

Normal body cells divide and multiply a certain number of times, and then stop because they are controlled by hormones and other body chemicals. After working for some months or years, normal body cells are replaced by fresh young cells that do the same job.

Cancer is the name given to a disease caused by abnormal cells multiplying out of control. Cancer cells behave differently than normal cells as a result of mutations in the cells.

Cancer cells generally form a small lump of tissue, a tumor, which becomes larger and larger. As a tumor grows, cancer cells may spread to other parts of the body. When they settle in a new area, the cells continue to multiply and may form another tumor. The cancer invades several parts of the body in this way. A growing tumor may press against various body parts, such as nerves and blood vessels, or it may eat into them causing serious damage and, if it is not stopped, death.

More than 200 different types of cancer affect various parts of the body. The most common forms of cancer in adults are lung cancer, prostate cancer, colorectal cancer, and breast cancer. Leukemia is a form of cancer affecting white blood cells, which are made in the bone marrow.

What causes cancer?

Smoking causes about one third of cancer cases. Diet is an important factor in causing another third of cancers. Some of the remaining third of cancers may be caused by viruses, chemicals in the workplace, or asbestos, but the cause of many cancers is unknown.

Who is at risk?

People in middle or old age are most vulnerable to cancer. Two thirds of cancer cases occur in people who are over 65 years old. But children and young people sometimes develop certain rare types of cancer.

One in three people will be diagnosed with cancer at some time in their lives, but only one in four deaths are caused by cancer. There are now many ways of treating cancer with surgery, drugs, and radiotherapy. People may sometimes live for many years after a diagnosis of cancer and eventually die of another disease.

These cancer cells, taken from a human bowel, have been magnified about 4,000 times.

Cancer Throughout History

Ancient records

Cancer is as old as civilization. Ancient Egyptian records describe eight cases of cancer of the breast in about 1600 B.C.E. These tumors were treated with what the ancient Egyptians called the fire drill—a red-hot poker used to cauterize, or seal, a bleeding wound.

The Greek physician, Hippocrates, known as the father of medicine, used the words *carcinos* and *carcinoma* to describe tumors. These words come from the Greek for crab, and probably refer to leg-like projections that seem to spread from a tumor, suggesting the shape of a crab.

Microscopes developed in the 19th century enabled doctors to see cancer cells for the first time.

Scientific investigations

The first scientific investigations of cancer were undertaken by the physician Giovanni Morgagni in Padua, Italy, in 1761. He dissected the bodies of people who had died of cancer and was able to relate their illness to the position and nature of the tumor. The first doctor to take a modern approach to cancer was the Scottish surgeon John Hunter (1728–1793). He suggested a method by which surgeons should decide whether or not to operate. He advised that a tumor could be removed if it was moveable and could be separated from surrounding tissues.

Microscopes

With the development of the modern microscope in the 19th century, doctors were able to study tumors in detail for the first time. In 1838 the German pathologist Johannes Muller showed that cancers are composed of cells like other body tissues. Another German, Rudolf Virchow (1821–1902), sometimes called the founder of cellular pathology, pioneered the identification of different types of cancer using the microscope. This was the foundation of modern diagnosis.

Surgery

Cancer surgery could not develop effectively until there were reliable methods of providing anesthesia and preventing infection. In 1865 Joseph Lister began the use of sterile instruments and other techniques for avoiding infections following surgery. Simple methods of anesthesia were developed at about the same time. Improvements in cancer surgery began to follow.

Radiotherapy

X-rays were discovered in 1895 by Wilhelm Röntgen, a Dutchman living in Germany. Radium, the radioactive material used in certain treatments, was discovered in 1898 by Marie Curie, a Polish woman working in Paris. The first attempts at radiotherapy were made a few years later, and by 1922 radiation was established as a method of treating cancer.

Chemotherapy

Drug treatment of cancer, or chemotherapy, began in the 1940s. As part of the U.S. military program, Alfred Gilman and Louis Goodman working at Yale University injected a solution of mustard gas (used as a weapon in World War I) into a mouse with cancer. The cancer disappeared and the first experiments with drugs on human cancer began shortly afterwards.

Rudolf Virchow identified malignant (cancerous) cells and began the scientific diagnosis of cancer.

Tar and smoke

Prior to the 19th century, small boys as young as five years old were put to work cleaning chimneys. The boys were bribed or beaten into climbing inside small flues, inaccessible to adults, and sweeping out the black soot. In 1775 Sir Percival Potts, a surgeon at St. Bartholomew's Hospital in London, described a cancer that was found on the scrotums of boys and men who worked as chimney sweeps. The cancer was originally diagnosed as a type of sexually transmitted disease, but Potts said this was mistaken.

Chimney sweeps in other countries, such as Germany, did not suffer from cancer of the scrotum as frequently. The Germans apparently wore better protective clothing and washed more thoroughly after work. It took another one hundred years for doctors to realize that the chimney sweeps' scrotal cancer was not only caused by soot but also by tar, paraffin, and other mineral oils.

In 1915 scientists at Tokyo University, Japan, put coal tar on the skin of rabbits. The rabbits developed cancer as a result. Scientists eventually realized that all kinds of tar-containing substances can alter genetic material and cause normal cells to develop into cancer cells. These observations and others led (in 1950) to the connection being made between smoking and lung cancer. Cigarette smoke consists of a fine mist of yellow tar that is deposited in the lungs and mouth where it may change normal cells into cancer cells.

Viruses

Other causes of cancer have been known for many years. In 1911 a virus that caused cancer in chickens was recognized by Peyton Rous at the Rockefeller Institute in New York. A number of viruses infecting people have been linked with cancer since that discovery. Cancers of the female genital area and of the penis are thought to be caused by a human virus called papilloma. HIV, the virus that causes AIDS, is associated with an increased risk of developing two cancers called Kaposi's sarcoma and non-Hodgkin's lymphoma.

The dangers of tobacco smoke were not understood until after 1950. Prior to this, many people, such as former British prime minister Stanley Baldwin (shown here on the right), did not realize the health risks associated with smoking.

How Cancer Grows and Spreads

Cancer occurs when the hereditary material (DNA) of normal body cells changes, allowing the cells to continue to divide without control. Unlike normal cells, cancer cells continue to multiply and reproduce indefinitely, so they outlive normal cells. Eventually the cancer cells form a tumor that consists of billions of abnormal cells.

Cancer cells do not stick together like normal cells, so individual cancer cells or small clumps of them easily drift away from the tumor. Cancer cells move throughout the body in the blood or in the lymph, the clear fluid that circulates throughout the body in the lymph ducts. Tumor cells tend to travel from the original, or primary, tumor to the nearest lymph glands—so this is the first place doctors generally look for signs of spreading.

Secondary tumors

Cancer may spread locally in the immediate area around the primary tumor. Growths may push out from the primary tumor or small groups of cells may metastasize—break off from the primary tumor and form what is called a secondary tumor, secondary growth, or metastasis. Cancer may, for example, spread from the ovary, which lies at the back of the abdomen (body cavity), to other parts of the abdomen. Lung cancer may spread to the pleura, the lining of the chest. Often the tumor cells also spread to other places, forming secondary tumors in places such as the liver, lungs, bones, or brain.

Cancer cells multiply to form lumps like this breast cancer tumor (center), made up of many abnormal cells.

Doctors examine MRI scans. These detailed images allow doctors to accurately pinpoint the position of a tumor.

How quickly does cancer spread?

Some cancers, such as colorectal cancer, grow relatively slowly and do not spread quickly. So there is a good chance that colorectal cancer will not have spread if it is spotted early. If it has not spread the tumor can be removed by surgery and the patient will be completely cured. Other cancers, such as lung cancer, grow relatively rapidly and are not often caught at an early stage when a complete cure is possible.

A tumor often does not cause any problems until it has reached a size that can be easily seen. Even then it may not cause immediate problems. A tumor eventually becomes so large that it interferes with the working of some part of the body, such as by blocking or partially blocking the bowel. By that time the cancer has usually been growing in the body for several years.

13

Signs and Symptoms of Cancer

Often the first sign of cancer is not a visible lump, but a symptom that might easily be blamed on something else. A hoarse voice or headache usually go away after a few days, but when they do not go away and show no signs of improving within a few days a doctor should be consulted. These symptoms could be the first sign of something more serious. Sometimes they may be the first sign of cancer. Bowel pain, blood in the feces, or unexplained weight loss may alert doctors to colorectal cancer. Lung cancer may only be detected when blood is found in the saliva, or when a person is tested for a chest infection or unexplained weight loss.

The first sign of breast cancer is often a small lump that may be felt with the fingers or detected on an X-ray. The vast majority of lumps in the body are not cancer, but a new lump that does not go away after several days should always be examined by a doctor. Lumps may have many causes. For example, a lump may be caused by a harmless fluid-filled sac or cyst, or by a small gland that is temporarily swollen as a result of infection.

A doctor will give advice about persistent problems that might be a sign of cancer.

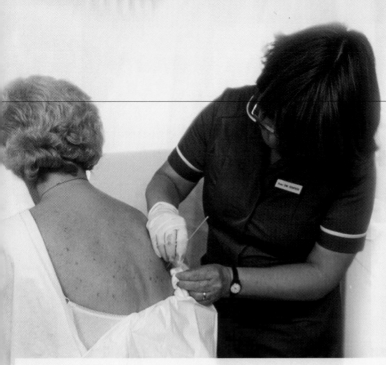

A nurse removes a mole from a woman's back. Once it has been removed, tests will be able to show whether or not it is malignant.

Warning signs of cancer

If a person develops one or more of the signs below, it does not necessarily mean the person has cancer. But a doctor should be consulted if the symptoms persist.

Type of cancer	Warning signs
Colorectal	persistent diarrhea/constipation or a combination of the two; blood in the feces; unexplained weight loss
Brain	headaches (but many people get these and they don't have cancer); weakness in limbs; slurred speech; personality changes
Breast	painless lump; bleeding or discharge from a nipple; change in breast size or shape
Leukemia	fatigue; lots of infections; increased bruising; bleeding gums
Lung	persistent cough; chest/shoulder pain; difficulty in breathing; hoarse voice; blood in the saliva; unexplained weight loss; repeated chest infection
Prostate	delay in flow when passing urine; reduced speed of urine flow; dribbling urine; pain on passing urine; blood in urine
Skin	a mole that enlarges, bleeds, itches, changes appearance, or becomes an irregular shape; color is important: moles should normally be one color, more than two colors in a mole is suspicious; sores that don't heal after three weeks

Diagnosis of Cancer

People usually see a doctor if they have a symptom such as a persistent hoarse voice or discomfort in the bowel and change of bowel habit. A series of tests must then be performed before the doctor is able to determine the cause of the problem.

There are three main types of tests for all cancers: imaging, cytology, and chemical tests.

Imaging

Images of the inside parts of the body obtained by X-rays are one of the most common ways of diagnosing cancer. Better X-rays can be obtained of the bowel, for example, if a person swallows barium. The barium reflects the X-rays and makes the bowel show up very clearly. X-ray examination of the breast, known as mammography, enables lumps to be found that are too small to feel.

X-rays or other methods can also be used to produce cross-sectional pictures created by computer. These CT, MRI, and PET scans enable very accurate location of a tumor. Images may also be obtained by use of ultrasound and by use of radioactive substances (radionuclides).

Cytology

Cytology is the study of cells under the microscope. A small sample, or biopsy, is taken from the suspect tissue and specially prepared for examination under the microscope. The sample may be taken with a needle or, in the case of the cervix (the neck of the womb), a sample of cells may be gently scraped off using a plastic scraper. A specialist can determine whether or not they are malignant by viewing the cells under the microscope.

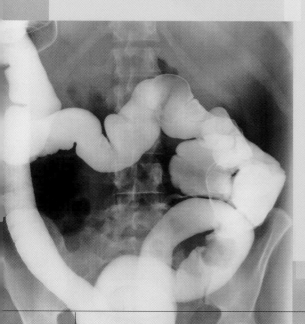

A barium meal is given to a patient before an X-ray of the bowel is taken. The barium reflects X-rays and makes the bowel and the tumor (lower right of the picture) show up better.

16

Chemical tests

In chemical tests, a sample of urine, feces, blood, or other body tissue is taken and tested for the presence of certain chemicals. The presence of a chemical may suggest that cancer is a possibility. Chemical tests may be used to determine if there is a problem that cannot easily be detected in other ways. Feces may, for example, be examined for hidden blood. If hidden blood is present there must be bleeding into the bowel, which could be caused by a tumor.

❝I find myself more comfortable telling people: 'I was diagnosed with cancer' instead of saying: 'I have cancer.' On some deep level I do not want to own this illness.❞

(Breast cancer survivor)

A woman lies with her head in an MRI scanner. The scan on the screen will show if she has a tumor in the brain.

17

Screening Tests

Cancer can be treated most effectively when it is detected and identified before it has spread to other parts of the body. This may be done with screening tests. These tests can find cancer when a person is still feeling completely well, years before the cancer might begin to make them ill. If a cancer can be detected at an early stage, the chance of treatment being effective is greater and the patient is more likely to make a full recovery.

The simplest form of screening is self-examination. Young men should examine their testes regularly and seek medical advice if an unusual lump is found. If it is detected early, testicular cancer can be treated more simply and effectively. If women examine their breasts regularly, an unusual lump may be detected early and a full medical examination may then be obtained. Screening for breast cancer with a mammogram (an X-ray of the breast) also enables the disease to be caught at an early stage, and simpler treatment can be given. Breast screening programs are generally limited to women over 45 or 50 who are at higher risk of developing breast cancer than younger women.

A mammogram (an X-ray of the breast) is taken to check for cancer.

Screening for cancer of the cervix (neck of the womb) has reduced the number of deaths from cervical cancer by about half. Screening tests are carried out by taking a sample of cells from the neck of the womb and examining them under a microscope. In this way the disease can be detected at an early stage and cured by surgical removal of the malignant cells.

When patients over the age of 60 are examined using a sigmoidoscope (a long flexible tube that can be used to examine the lower bowel), as many as 3 patients in 1,000 are found to have colorectal cancer. But the procedure is expensive and generally only used when some other symptom—such as blood in the feces—suggests a problem. Early detection greatly improves a person's chances of surviving bowel cancer.

Prostate cancer may also be detected using a blood test for prostate specific antigen (PSA). However, this screening test is controversial because many doctors do not consider it accurate enough. Some doctors argue that the test saves lives and are enthusiastic about screening for prostate cancer. Others argue against using the PSA test because it is not completely reliable.

No screening program is 100 percent accurate. Some people who have cancer will be missed and they may then have a false sense of security. Other people who do not have the disease are sometimes falsely diagnosed. These people suffer unnecessary treatment and needless anxiety.

A technician examines cells taken from the cervix (neck of the womb). Cancer cells have an unusual appearance.

LEICA 200

Food and Cancer

Experts broadly agree that about a third of cancer deaths are caused primarily by the food we eat. There are a few foods, such as certain types of salted fish eaten in China, or peanuts contaminated by growth of a fungus, that have been shown to cause cancer when consumed regularly over long periods. However, in most cases the risk of cancer seems to be increased not by eating one particular food but rather by the combination of ingredients in the diet as a whole. The risk of cancer can be reduced by diets that are low in fat and high in fiber, high in vegetables and fruits, and high in grain products such as bread, cereals, and pasta.

Fat

Cancer of the breast, bowel, and prostate have been linked to diets that are high in fat and oil, such as from cooking oils and fat in meat and dairy products. Countries that have a high consumption of fat have a higher proportion of these cancers in the population. The type of fat does not seem to be as important as the total quantity of fat that is eaten.

Alcohol

Taking more than three alcoholic drinks per day is linked to an increase in the risk of developing cancer, particularly cancer of the mouth, throat, and esophagus. Taking more than six drinks per day is associated with a 60 percent increase in the average risk of cancer.

Obesity

People who are obese (seriously overweight) have an increased risk of certain cancers including those of the breast, womb, bowel, kidney, esophagus, stomach, and gallbladder.

Vegetables and fruits

Diets that are low in vegetables and fruits are believed to increase the risk of certain forms of cancer, including cancer of the lung, bowel, breast, mouth, stomach, and ovaries. Vegetables and fruits contain substances that protect against cancer, including fiber, vitamins A and C, and carotenoids (the yellow and red substances found in carrots, melons, and dark green vegetables). This has led to campaigns for people to eat five servings of vegetables and fruits per day—a serving is one average sized apple, pear, orange, or banana or two small fruits such as kiwis or plums, or an equivalent amount of vegetables.

Fiber

Fiber is the part of food that is not digested in the human body. Fiber is found in grain products and in vegetables and fruits. A high consumption of whole grains, taken as wholegrain bread or breakfast cereal, appears to protect against cancer of the bowel.

Cancer and Smoking

Smoking causes the deaths of hundreds of thousands of people every year all over the world. They die not just of various types of cancer but also of heart disease and strokes. One third of all cancers are caused by smoking.

Lung cancer accounts for more than a quarter of all deaths from cancer, and most lung cancer is caused by smoking. Cigarette smoke can cause cancer of all the parts of the body it comes into contact with except for the fingers. It causes cancer of the larynx (voice box), the inside of the mouth, the tongue, the lips, and the esophagus (the tube taking food to the stomach).

The risk of developing cancer depends on how much a person smokes—the more a person smokes the greater their chance of developing cancer. The younger a person is when they start to smoke the greater their risk of developing cancer. People who give up smoking greatly reduce their risk of dying of cancer caused by tobacco.

It is now recognized that passive smoking (breathing in tobacco smoke from the air) is a significant cause of lung cancer in non-smokers. A person who works next to a smoker or lives in a house where people smoke may have their risk of developing lung cancer increased by between 30 and 50 percent.

Treatment of lung cancer

Current treatment of lung cancer is not very effective, although some advances are being made. There are several different types of lung cancer, and a patient's future depends on the type and the stage of the cancer. Surgery is possible in some patients with lung cancer, and these patients probably have the best chance of long-term survival. Radiotherapy and chemotherapy are the more common forms of treatment. These produce good short-term results over a period of six months to two years and long-term survival is possible.

Suffering the consequences

Deborah Norton began smoking at the age of 12 and at 47 discovered she had cancer of the larynx. A month later she had her larynx completely removed and now breathes through a tube in her neck. She says "No one wants to live like this out of choice. But, it was a choice I made without realizing the consequences. If I can help just one person to stop smoking, I will continue to speak out."

"[Smoking is] the chief single, avoidable cause of death in our society and the most important public health issue of our time."

(C. Everett Koop, former U.S. surgeon general)

23

Breast Cancer

Breast cancer is most often detected as a small lump in the breast. Frequently it is found by the woman herself, but it may be picked up on an X-ray during screening (mammography). Other than skin cancer, breast cancer is the most common form of cancer in women. It is a devastating diagnosis for a woman—but better treatment and earlier detection have led to an improvement in the survival rate of women with breast cancer over the last twenty years.

What causes breast cancer?

It is not known exactly what causes breast cancer, but certain conditions and lifestyles have been found to increase the risk of breast cancer. For example, women have an increased risk of breast cancer if they drink between two and five alcoholic drinks a day, if they are overweight, or if they put on a lot of weight as an adult. The risk of breast cancer is also greater for women who have close relatives who had the disease before the age of 50.

Treatment

Operations to treat breast cancer attempt to remove the tumor in the breast to prevent further spread of the cancer. The type of operation will depend on how advanced the cancer is. If the tumor is at an early stage, a removal of the lump with a small amount of surrounding tissue (called a lumpectomy) is carried out. However, if the cancer has begun to spread from the breast then a radical

The pink ribbon is the symbol worn by people who support breast cancer awareness and research.

mastectomy is likely to be carried out. This involves the removal of the entire breast as well as some of the lymph glands in the armpit.

Operations are generally followed by radiotherapy, chemotherapy, and/or hormone therapy to kill any remaining cancer cells in the area of the breast. The hormone drug Tamoxifen is generally given for about five years after surgery to help prevent the cancer from returning.

Doctors monitor a woman who is recovering from an operation to remove a tumor from the breast.

Non-cancerous lumps

Ideally a woman should examine her breasts every month to look for any change. If a change is detected or there is a discharge or blood coming from the nipple she should consult a doctor. Eight out of ten breast lumps are not cancer. They may be the result of fibrocystic disease. In this disease one or both breasts become lumpy and tender in the week or so before a period begins. The lumps are caused by harmless fluid-filled sacs. Lumps in the breast may also form because of fibroadenoma. These are harmless rubbery growths that can be moved around under the skin and cause no pain.

Leukemia

Leukemia is the most common cancer in children but it also occurs in adults. It is a cancer of the white blood cells, which are made in the bone marrow in the center of bones. White blood cells are important for defending the body against infections. But people with leukemia have abnormally large numbers of white cells in their blood. There may be so many of them that they do not leave sufficient space for the red blood cells, which are necessary to carry oxygen from the lungs throughout the body. They also do not leave space in the bone marrow for other normal cells.

Types of leukemia

There are many different types of leukemia. They are named according to the cells they are derived from in the bone marrow—the lymphocytes or the myelocytes—and according to whether the leukemia is chronic or acute. In acute leukemia the white blood cells divide rapidly but do not mature properly. In chronic leukemia the cells look normal but live longer than normal and build up in the blood.

This boy with leukemia has lost all of his hair following drug treatment to kill cancer cells.

White blood cells (the light-colored cells) from a person with leukemia have become malignant (cancerous) and multiplied, leaving little space for normal red blood cells (dark pink).

What causes leukemia?

Leukemia is sometimes caused by exposure to radiation or chemicals that damage DNA, the hereditary material of the cell. Workers in atomic power plants, for example, are at risk. For this reason they are strictly regulated so that they do not spend too much time exposed to radiation. However, the damage to DNA most often occurs accidentally during periods of rapid cell growth when the DNA is being copied very frequently. The more that cells multiply the greater the chance of an error occurring in the copying of DNA.

Treatment of leukemia

Treatment of leukemia in children is generally very successful. About 75 percent of children now survive five or more years after the illness began.

Treatment varies according to the type of leukemia. At first, drugs (chemotherapy) are given to kill as many of the cancer cells as possible and induce a remission—a temporary reduction in the severity of the disease when the number of cancer cells has been greatly reduced. After a short rest to give the patient time to recover, more drugs are given to rid the body of the last few cancer cells. This may be followed by radiotherapy to kill cancer cells that remain in the bone marrow. This treatment is sufficient to cure many patients. If the disease returns again, a bone marrow transplant may be possible if a suitable donor can be found.

Skin Cancer

Skin cancer is the most common form of cancer. There are two major types: melanoma, which accounts for only about 4 percent of skin cancer cases but 80 percent of skin cancer deaths, and non-melanoma skin cancer. Any new growth on the skin, a spot or lump that is getting larger, or a sore that does not heal in three months, might be skin cancer and should be examined by a doctor.

Melanoma

Melanoma is generally first noticed as a dark spot on the skin resembling a mole. A normal mole is an evenly colored brown, black, or tan spot on the skin that may be flat or raised and may be round or oval. Normal moles generally stay the same size for many years. Melanoma forms a much more irregular spot. Occasionally a normal mole may develop into melanoma.

Non-melanoma skin cancer

Non-melanoma skin cancers are generally spotted early and are easily treated. They usually appear on parts of the body—such as the head and neck, lips, and the backs of the hands—that are most frequently exposed to the sun. Theses cancers grow relatively slowly and rarely spread far.

A hat and sunscreen applied to the most exposed body parts protects against burning and skin cancer.

Safety in the sun

Extensive exposure to strong sunlight, particularly when it leads to sunburn, increases the risk of skin cancer. People who work outdoors and have fair or light skin are most at risk. They need to wear suitable clothing and a hat to protect themselves from sunburn. They should also use sunscreen (with a sun protection factor, or SPF, of fifteen or more), although this is not as effective as clothing and a hat.

While care must be taken to avoid sunburn, it is important not to avoid sunlight completely. Exposure of the skin to sunlight for about ten minutes per day is desirable to ensure a good supply of vitamin D, which is believed to protect against certain cancers including melanoma.

This is a close up of a melanoma. This type of skin cancer generally appears as a dark or multi-colored spot on the skin.

Warning signs of melanoma

It is important to examine moles on the skin and look for any changes. If any of the following are observed, a doctor should be consulted to check whether the mole is normal:

- One half of the mole does not match the other half
- The edges of the mole are ragged or notched
- The color of the mole is not the same all over
- The mole is wider than about one-quarter inch (six millimeters)
- The mole has changed in size or appearance.

Cancer in Children

Children rarely get cancer and when they do they can often be cured. Nevertheless cancer is the most common cause of death other than accidents in children under fourteen years of age.

The most common form of cancer in children is leukemia, which accounts for about one third of all cancer cases in children. Brain tumors, which are relatively rare in adults, are the second most common childhood cancer.

Some childhood cancers begin while the baby is still in the womb, although they may not be noticed until the child is several years old. These embryonal cancers arise from cells that have failed to develop in the normal way and eventually become malignant. Examples of such embryonal cancers are retinoblastoma, which occurs in the eye, and hepatoblastoma, which occurs in the liver.

Children have fun playing a computer game in a hospital. Today most children with cancer have a good chance of a full recovery.

Treatment of childhood cancer

Cancers that affect children tend to be sensitive to drugs and so very good results are obtained in treating cancer in children. In the 1960s, before the introduction of modern chemotherapy, children with cancer could not be treated effectively and most of them died. Today the drugs used in chemotherapy are combined in various ways and much better results are obtained, with about 70 percent of children who have had cancer surviving into adulthood.

Chemotherapy rapidly produces remission of the disease, but the treatment needs to be repeated several times and may be combined with surgery or radiotherapy to ensure that all malignant cells in the body are destroyed. Treatment can last more than a year and success varies with the type of cancer.

Treatment is often given in highly specialized cancer centers, where doctors and nurses have accumulated experience of the best way to use these powerful drugs and staff members know how to help the children through a very difficult time.

Cancer is not an infectious disease

Occasionally two children in the same school, or the same neighborhood, or even in the same family develop cancer. When these cases have been investigated they have generally been found to occur together by chance. Parents often feel guilty and try to think of things they did which might have caused a child to develop cancer. The cause of childhood cancers is not known, though, and parents should not blame themselves.

Treating Cancer

Surgery

Surgery is often the best way to remove a tumor and, if cancer cells have not spread, surgery is likely to result in a complete cure. Surgery may not be possible if the tumor is large or awkwardly placed or if the cancer has spread locally to involve a large area of tissue.

In order to have the best chance of removing every bit of the cancer, the surgeon will generally remove a wide band of tissue from around the tumor, or remove all of the affected organ together with the tumor. The surgeon will generally remove local lymph glands and lymph ducts near the tumor. This is because the lymph glands are generally the first place that small groups of cells that break away from the main tumor will settle. There are many lymph glands in the body, so the removal of a few does not have a serious effect on the body's defense against infection.

Surgery is often followed by treatment with radiotherapy or drugs (chemotherapy). This is done in order to kill any cancer cells that have spread to other parts of the body and have not been removed by the surgeon. These therapies are sometimes given before surgery in order to shrink the tumor and induce remission, making surgery easier.

Pain-killing drugs are given after the operation to make the patient more comfortable and to enable the patient to move around more easily. It is important for patients to move around as soon as possible after surgery in order to prevent chest infections and dangerous blood clots.

Skating to recovery

Molly McMaster was told she had cancer on her 23rd birthday. She was an ice-skating teacher and hockey coach and dreamed of playing one day for the U.S. women's hockey team. But she became sick and was forced to return home to Glen Falls, New York. She had emergency surgery and 23 inches (60 centimeters) of her colon were removed together with a large tumor. "I was in really good physical shape when I went into this and I think that it helped," said Molly. Following the surgery and chemotherapy treatment, Molly skated from Glen Falls to Greeley, Colorado, on a 71-day, 2,000-mile trip to raise money for cancer research.

Surgeons remove a prostate gland that contains a tumor. Prostate cancer is a common cancer in older men.

Chemotherapy

Chemotherapy is the medical name given to the treatment of cancer with drugs. Chemotherapy may cure a cancer or it may be used to reduce the size of the cancer and induce remission. A complete course of chemotherapy usually takes several months. It may be given before or after surgery or radiotherapy, or it may be given by itself.

The drugs used in chemotherapy are only able to kill cancer cells when they are dividing, so cancer cells that are not dividing at the time of treatment will survive. By the time the next treatment starts some of these resting cells will have started to divide and they will then be killed. Normal body cells that are dividing at the time of treatment are killed in the same way as the cancer cells. However, there are many more normal body cells than cancer cells, and normal body cells are generally more robust. So the cancer cells are eliminated while most of the body cells survive.

Side effects

Chemotherapy drugs cause a lot of damage to body cells and tissues, and it is normal to feel very tired while undergoing this treatment. The body is also short of white blood cells since they divide frequently and so many are killed during chemotherapy. This means that the body is less resistant to infection.

A doctor discusses treatment with a patient who has leukemia. Treatment may take months and needs to be planned to allow for rest periods.

The hair and the skin are growing constantly. Cells lining the digestive system are constantly replacing themselves and cells in the bone marrow are also growing very actively to replace blood cells. Since chemotherapy kills normal cells that are dividing, these are the parts of the body that are most severely affected by chemotherapy. The main side effects are fatigue, nausea, vomiting, a sore mouth, increased risk of infection, and loss of hair. These side effects will stop once the treatment ends and the hair will then grow back.

Some cancer drugs cause infertility, which may be temporary or permanent. Before treatment begins, men may put some of their sperm into a sperm bank, where it can be stored for later use, and women may sometimes put their eggs or tissue from their ovaries into storage. They may then be able to have children at a later date when they are ready to start a family.

A hospital pharmacist prepares a cancer drug in a special cabinet designed to make sure the drug is not contaminated.

Radiotherapy

Radiotherapy uses a beam of radiation, usually X-rays, to destroy cancer cells. The beam is focused on a tumor or area of tissue to concentrate the energy in one place. Radiotherapy beams use a much higher quantity of energy than an X-ray. Treatment is often repeated over a period of several weeks.

The radiation damages the DNA of the cancer cells and makes it impossible for them to continue to grow. Normal cells are also damaged, but there are more of them and they are generally better able to repair themselves. Healthy body tissue can be shielded from the effects of radiation with a special apron containing sheets of lead.

Radiotherapy is particularly useful in the treatment of cancer in areas that have a complicated structure that may make them unsuitable for surgery—such as the tongue, the throat, or the brain. Radiation is also a convenient way of treating cancer of the skin, the breast, or the cervix since other tissues or organs are not in the way and side effects are therefore minimal.

Radiation treatment may also be delivered to a small area by means of a radioactive implant. In this method, the implant—a small pellet or a wire of radioactive material (radium, uranium, or cobalt 60)—is placed into the tumor and left there for a few days. Gamma rays emitted by the implant destroy the surrounding tissue. This method is often used to treat cancer of the tongue, the womb, and the cervix.

Radiotherapy may also be given orally as a medicine. Radioactive iodine may be given, for example, to treat cancer of the thyroid gland. First, surgeons remove as much of the gland as possible. Then radioactive iodine is given as a drink. Any remaining cells from the thyroid gland pick up the iodine. The iodine then releases radiation, destroying the remaining thyroid cells, with minimal damage to nearby tissues. Normal cells are not affected by the iodine and remain unchanged.

Side effects

Radiotherapy treatments are painless in themselves but they do have side effects. Fatigue is the most common side effect. Radiotherapy frequently causes skin irritation and a temporary change of skin color in the area affected by the radiation beam. Hair may also be lost when the beam of radiation crosses the scalp, but will grow back again. Radiotherapy may have to be repeated after a rest period to ensure that all cancer cells are killed.

A radiotherapy machine is aimed at a patient's head using laser cross hairs to make sure the radiation hits the target—a tumor in the brain.

Transplants

A new generation of cancer treatments has been developed in the last decade. These methods have not in any way replaced the tried and tested methods of surgery, radiotherapy, and chemotherapy, but they have enabled some cancers to be treated that could not be treated before. Surgeons are now able to remove organs from one person, the donor, and transplant them into another person—such as when a person's kidneys have stopped working. Transplants of bone marrow or blood cells are being used as part of the treatment of certain types of cancer.

Bone marrow transplants may be used to treat leukemia. Bone marrow contains stem cells that constantly divide to produce white blood cells, which defend the body against infection. The stem cells may become malignant and then give rise to leukemic cells. Conventional radiotherapy and chemotherapy treatments are used to kill the malignant stem cells and this is sufficient to cure many people who have leukemia. If this treatment fails, a transplant may be possible.

When a transplant has been arranged, heavier doses of chemotherapy can be given to kill the remaining malignant stem cells. But all the normal stem cells are killed at the same time. So a donor, with carefully matched cells, must be available who can provide normal bone marrow cells to be transplanted into the patient. The donor marrow is given to the patient in the same way as a blood transfusion.

A patient is being prepared for a transplant. Stem cells are collected that will be returned to the patient following high-dose chemotherapy.

Breast and ovarian cancer are sometimes treated in a similar way, with very heavy doses of drugs that, as a side effect, kill all the cells in the bone marrow. Before giving this heavy drug treatment, stem cells are taken from the patient's own blood and stored. After the drug treatment is completed, these stored stem cells are returned to the patient.

However, bone marrow and stem cell transplants carry risks. Following the procedure, it takes at least two weeks for white blood cells to begin to be active again and much longer for the patient's resistance to infection to return to normal. There is also a risk that the transplanted cells will fail to grow because they are rejected by the body.

Despite these problems, bone marrow transplants have been accepted as successful because the chance of a cure is high for the large majority who survive the first two years after the transplant.

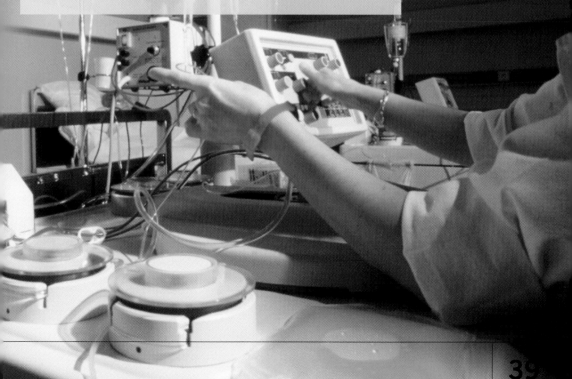

Alex's Story

Alex Harris is a financial analyst with a passion for bicycle riding. But he thought his cycling days might be over when he found a painful bump on his shin and learned it was cancer.

Now he is more determined than ever to get on his bike.

"I had a goal, and the goal was to go out to Texas and ride in the Ride for the Roses cycle race and complete it. That's kind of what got me through I guess, just being stubborn and having a goal," said Alex who lives in Huntsville, Alabama. The race was inspired by champion bike racer Lance Armstrong, who won the Tour de France cycle race five years in a row after recovering from testicular cancer.

Alex's doctors told him that the standard treatment for his cancer, a rare type of sarcoma, was a bone graft and chemotherapy, but they were not going to recommend them because the statistics did not show that they worked. Nevertheless they hoped to save his leg with a course of radiotherapy.

Alex had six weeks of radiotherapy and five operations. The first operation removed the tumor. But his progress was complicated by an infection of the bone and three more operations were needed.

Nothing was simple. Alex had an allergic reaction to the antibiotic drugs he was being given, and he was given some 60 treatments with hyperbaric oxygen—oxygen under pressure in a special chamber. But he came through them all and was finally able to compete in the Ride for the Roses.

Alex says that cancer has given him a new appreciation of life. When there is a moment of joy he grasps it, relishes it, and does not let it go. There was one of those moments on a recent cycle ride.

"We were rolling through a neighborhood and passed a house with two little girls playing in the backyard. One was bouncing on a trampoline and the other was spraying her with a hose. I can still hear the squeals of laughter," said Alex. "A year ago I would never have recognized how beautiful that sound is, much less remembered it."

"I guess having cancer changed me for the better. I wish I could have changed a different way, but I'll take it this way if necessary."

(Alex Harris)

Anxieties and Fears

When a person is diagnosed as having cancer he or she will often experience anxiety that can be very severe. Anxiety may make the pain experienced by cancer sufferers feel worse. It may also disturb sleep, increase fatigue, and delay a full recovery. Anxiety can also be a major factor in nausea and vomiting. Anxiety, though, is a normal response to stressful events and is part of the process of coming to terms with an illness.

Fear of the unknown

Fear of the unknown is often a significant cause of anxiety. Patients may feel less anxious when they are given more information about their illness and their treatment, or when they find out more from brochures available from cancer support groups or websites. Patients also usually feel less nervous as they become more accustomed to seeing doctors and going to hospitals. They gradually feel more at ease and less threatened by fears of the unknown as they get to know the hospital staff.

Cancer forces young people to think about life and make difficult decisions.

Anxieties about treatment

Anxiety may also arise during the course of hospital treatment. Poorly controlled pain and severe side effects of treatment such as nausea and exhaustion may make a person nervous about more treatment. Discussions with medical staff will help greatly in these circumstances. Medical and nursing staff may suggest modifying the treatment schedule in some way. This gives the patient an important feeling of control, which in turn may reduce anxiety.

Relaxation

Relaxation is also important. The best way to relax varies greatly from one person to another. For one person, listening to music or playing board or card games with friends may be a good way. Talking with friends and family about ordinary things may be best for others. Special tapes or CDs designed to encourage relaxation can be very effective. Massage and aromatherapy are good ways for other people.

Signs of severe anxiety

Severe anxiety can be brought on by a diagnosis of cancer, or by other life events. Signs of severe anxiety include:

- intense fears
- inability to absorb information
- inability to co-operate with medical staff
- shortness of breath
- sweating
- trembling
- light-headedness or dizziness
- sensation of rapid heartbeat (palpitations).

Information about cancer and its treatment is available from hospitals and support groups.

Recovering from Brain Cancer

Matthew's story

One question concerned Matthew Zachary before he had surgery for a brain tumor. He did not ask his doctor: "Am I going to live?" Instead, he asked: "Am I going to be able to play the piano again?"

Matthew was 21 years old and studying for a music degree at Binghamton University, New York. He had struggled with a weakness in his left hand that threatened to prevent him from playing. Doctors thought at first it was carpel tunnel syndrome, irritation to a nerve in his wrist, caused by the demands of practicing piano 80 hours a week. But a few weeks later his speech became slurred and he had trouble walking.

A scan showed that Matthew had a tumor the size of a golf ball in the lower part of his brain. Two weeks later the tumor was removed surgically. When he got back home he found he could play the piano again. Without his piano playing Matthew had felt lost, now life was worthwhile once more. However, he could not play as he had before.

The operation on his brain had affected his ability to move his fingers and he had to retrain his left hand.

After his operation doctors gave Matthew only a 60 percent chance of living for five years. He had to return to the hospital for radiotherapy. The treatment made him very sick, but he worked through his feelings with jazz improvisation on the piano.

Matthew, with a lot of hard work, completed his degree. He was then advised to take a one-year course of chemotherapy in order to be sure that all the cancer cells were killed. But he asked some questions and found that the proposed drug treatment might damage nerves in his hands and could only be expected to add five months to his life.

"I would rather live to age 26 and die being able to play the piano, than live to 26 and a half and not be able to play," he said.

Matthew has since rebuilt his life and so far the cancer has not returned. He now plays the piano professionally and has starred in a number of charity events to raise money for cancer research.

> **"Everything that happens to you, whether you like it or not, becomes a part of your life. You must live your life and be the best you can be every step of the way."**
>
> (Matthew Zachary, pictured)

Friends and Family

Breaking bad news

It is not easy to tell people bad news. A person with cancer may not feel able to talk about their illness right away. It may take time for a person with cancer to absorb information about their illness and find the right words to tell others. Sometimes patients want their distress to be kept private, especially at the beginning. But it may come as a relief when friends and family do know. The person with cancer can then enjoy receiving greetings and visits from friends that provide what is often a vital lifeline.

Relaxation with friends and family is an important way of overcoming the stress of cancer treatment.

Links to a normal world

For people with cancer, friends and family are an important link with the normal world outside of the hospital. People with cancer want to feel that they are still actively connected and involved with this world even though the hospital room and treatment isolates them. Patients want to hear good and bad news of family and friends so they do not feel excluded.

Sharing feelings and listening

People with cancer often do not want advice. People who give advice often do not know all the circumstances, and even if they are well informed too much advice can just create additional worry. People with cancer often find it more helpful if friends and family ask questions and listen. Laughter and talking about other things will often help to make a person with cancer feel normal. Sometimes holding hands and crying together brings people closer and makes everyone feel better.

Baseball cap replaces hair

Michele Conley was told she would lose all her hair within three weeks of her first chemotherapy. Michele, 39, asked her children whether they would prefer her to wear a wig or a baseball cap. They voted for the baseball cap. But when her hair began to come out in fistfuls she started to wear a wig. She wasn't ready to look at herself in the mirror or let her children see her bald head. "A very feminine part of me was gone," said Michele. When she did show them her head, her children said: "Cool, you look like Michael Jordan." She felt free, and after that only wore the baseball cap.

> **"Being diagnosed with cancer accelerates your life. You appreciate the time you have. It's pulled my family more lovingly tight than we have ever been."**
>
> (Andy Cayton, cancer survivor)

Hospices and Palliative Care

Even when cancer cannot be cured, a person may still have a period of life ahead that may be better enjoyed with the right kind of help. Palliative care, which attempts to slow the cancer down and control any pain, will make it possible for a cancer patient to be more active and may provide months or even years of life.

Palliative care uses radiotherapy or chemotherapy to delay the growth of tumors when it is no longer possible to eradicate them entirely. However, cancer cells become resistant to radiotherapy and chemotherapy and these treatments tend to become increasingly ineffective.

When people with cancer become very ill and do not have long to live, they may enter a hospice or nursing home— a home that provides specialized care for sick people who are not expected to get better. The first modern hospice was founded in 1967 by Dame Cicely Saunders in London. It was based on ancient ideas of hospitality and charity. A hospice was originally a place of shelter and rest for weary and sick travellers. Now a hospice is a place where travellers at the end of life's journey may find peace.

Hospices have developed special knowledge and skill in controlling pain and in providing compassionate care. They try to help people enjoy their last days or weeks of life in dignity surrounded by their family and friends. They seek to treat the person rather than the disease and neither hasten death nor postpone it. Instead, they try to make life comfortable for the patient while allowing the patient to remain in control.

Hospice care also tries to help patients with their spiritual needs. This may mean arranging a suitable religious ceremony, or helping patients to come to terms with death and helping them to say goodbye to family and friends. The hospice team will also help friends and relatives work through the process of grieving. Hospices often have support groups where friends and relatives can meet others who have had similar experiences that all can share and seek to understand.

"Cancer has a way of making you take an inventory of your life. It has made some good changes in my life. I think that my husband and I are closer as a result."

(Delores, cancer survivor)

Caregivers help with pain control in a hospice—a place for people with cancer near the end of their lives.

49

Hope in the Fight Against Cancer

Researchers have made great progress in understanding cancer. New cancer cases and cancer deaths are falling overall. Screening tests for cancer of the breast and cancer of the cervix are bringing earlier diagnosis and treatment and are saving lives.

Hope in the fight against cancer

Scientists have found key genes in cancer cells that cause them to grow out of control, and they are beginning to understand why this happens. Eventually they will develop new drugs that will be able to prevent the growth of cancer cells more effectively.

Today, new drugs are just beginning to become available that make use of immune reactions to provide new ways of treating cancer. They include monoclonal antibodies and other forms of immune treatment such as cancer vaccines that are currently being tested for kidney, ovarian, breast, colon, and lung cancer. But these new vaccines are only available as part of trials, which are the most important way of finding out if new treatments work.

Success in the fight against cancer is shown by a falling rate of cancer deaths. Until the 1990s the rate of cancer deaths increased in the United States and Europe, and then it steadied or began to fall as a result of improvements in treatment, prevention, and screening. More than a quarter of all cancer deaths are caused by lung cancer and smoking, but the rate of death from lung cancer is falling, as are deaths from each of the other big killers: breast, colorectal, and prostate cancer.

A person who dies of cancer loses on average fifteen years of life—more years of life than are lost from any other disease including heart disease or strokes. Breast and colon cancer may strike at a relatively young age and, together with cancer in children, they are the most important causes of lost years of life. Progress has been made in understanding the link between food and cancer, but scientists still have much to learn. Effective ways will eventually be found to prevent cancer, as well as better ways of discovering it early and treating it with better targeted drugs that have fewer side effects.

"If it weren't for cancer I wouldn't have made the changes in my life that gave me the momentum and the courage to do things I never would have done."

(Jean Karotkin, Dallas, who had a mastectomy at age 38)

Jane Tomlinson has incurable breast cancer, but she has raised $75,000 for cancer research through her sporting achievements, including a marathon and a triathlon.

Information and Advice

A great deal of information about cancer is available on the web. General background information and detailed information about particular types of cancer or particular drugs can be found.

Contacts

The American Cancer Society
www.cancer.org
This organization provides well organized and detailed information about different cancers, cancer treatments and patients' problems.

The Cancer Survivors Network
www.acscsn.org
This is the American Cancer Society's free online support group for cancer survivors and loved ones who share their experiences on message boards.

Oncolink
www.oncolink.upenn.edu
This is a comprehensive information resource on cancer from the University of Pennsylvania, providing in-depth information on most types of cancer.

Candlelighters Childhood Cancer Foundation
www.candlelighters.org
This organization has a mission to educate, support and serve families of children with cancer and survivors of childhood cancer.

The Association of Cancer Online Resources
www.acor.org
Develops and supports Internet facilities for cancer patients and their families.

More Books to Read

Alagna, Magdalena. *Everything You Need to Know about Chemotherapy.*
   New York: Rosen Publishing, 2001.

Lamb, Kirsten. *Cancer.* Chicago, IL .:Raintree Publishers, 2002.

Martin, Carrie and Martin, Chia. *The Rainbow Feelings of Cancer: A Book of Children Who Have a Loved One With Cancer.* Prescott, AZ.: Hohm Press, 2001.

Stewart, Gail B. *Teens with Cancer.* Farmington Hills, Mich.: Gale Group, 2001.

Glossary

acute
severe medical conditions that appear suddenly

anesthesia
the state of insensitivity to pain caused by gases or drugs, especially before a surgical operation

benign
(of cells or tissues) not malignant or cancerous

biopsy
test involving removal of a small piece of tissue from the body

bone marrow
soft fatty tissue in the center of bones that produces all the cells in the blood

cellular pathology
branch of medicine that studies the nature of diseases by examining cells in the laboratory

chemotherapy
treatment of disease with drugs

chronic
persisting for a long time

colorectal
of the colon and/or rectum

CT scan (computerized tomography)
technique for displaying a cross-section through a human body using X-rays or ultrasound

cyst
abnormal lump or swelling filled with fluid

DNA
deoxyribonucleic acid, the hereditary material that carries genes in every cell of the body

gamma rays
type of radiation that comes, for example, from the radioactive material cobalt 60

gene
small unit of hereditary material that carries the instruction for building a protein or some other part of an organism

genetic material
another name for DNA

hormone
chemical substance that is released into the body in one place and has an effect in another place

hormone therapy
treatment with hormones or drugs very similar to hormones

immune reaction
reaction of the body's immune system to something in the body such as an infection or growth of malignant tissue

Kaposi's sarcoma
malignant skin tumor, which may occur in association with AIDS but also separately

leukemia
type of cancer in which white blood cells multiply out of control

lymph
milky fluid containing white blood cells that collects in spaces between cells in the body

lymph ducts
tubes that carry lymph from the tissues back to the blood stream

lymph glands
(also called lymph nodes) small pieces of tissue that are responsible for the immune reactions of the body and provide defense against infection

malignant
(of cells or tissues) cancerous

mammography
technique that uses X-rays to detect breast tumors

mastectomy
surgical operation to remove a breast

melanoma
dark-colored mole that contains malignant tissue; the most serious form of skin cancer

monoclonal antibody
special type of antibody, created in a laboratory, which may be used in treating cancer

MRI scan (magnetic resonance imaging)
form of imaging which uses high-frequency radio waves in a strong magnetic field

mutation
change in a gene

non-Hodgkin's lymphoma
any cancer of lymph tissue other than Hodgkin's lymphoma (a type of cancer involving the lymph glands)

non-melanoma skin cancer
any type of skin cancer other than melanoma

palliative
type of care focusing on alleviating pain rather than curing disease

PET scan (positron emission tomography)
form of imaging used especially for scanning the brain

prostate
gland located under the bladder in men, which makes the fluid part of semen

radioactive implant
small piece of material, such as wire, that is inserted into a tumor and produces radioactivity that kills off surrounding cells

radiotherapy
treatment with X-rays or other types of radiation

remission
temporary reduction in severity of disease

sarcoma
cancer of connective tissue, the tissue that surrounds organs and holds different parts of the body together

screening test
test to determine if someone has a cancer that they do not know about

sexually transmitted disease
disease that infects someone as a result of sexual intercourse or other sexual activity

stem cells
cells present in many tissues of the body that give rise to more specialized cells typical of a particular tissue

thyroid gland
gland located in the front of the neck that regulates the body's energy level

transfusion
transfer of blood or other fluid into a person's body

tumor
lump or piece of tissue that is malignant; or a swelling that may be malignant (cancerous) or benign (not malignant)

ultrasound
sound that cannot be heard by the human ear, used in medicine to produce images of internal parts of the body

white blood cells
cells in the blood that defend the body against infection

Index